God's
THROUGH THE EYES OF
Child

A Psychiatric Survivor's Success Story

GLENDYN KESTER

THROUGH THE EYES OF GOD'S CHILD
Copyright © 2013 by Glendyn Kester

Scripture taken from The Holy Bible, New International Version®, NIV® Copyright © 1973, 1978, 1984, 2011 by Biblica, Inc.™ Used by permission. All rights reserved worldwide.

ISBN: 978-1-77069-761-4

Word Alive Press
131 Cordite Road, Winnipeg, MB R3W 1S1
www.wordalivepress.ca

WORD ALIVE PRESS
Just Write!

Library and Archives Canada Cataloguing in Publication

Kester, Glendyn Norma, 1958-
     Through the eyes of God's child / Glendyn Norma Kester.

ISBN 978-1-77069-761-4

     1. Kester, Glendyn Norma, 1958-. 2. Christian biography--Canada. I. Title.

BR1725.K47A3 2012   277.1'083092   C2012-907158-7

For my mother,
With love

"Let us remember what we are here for to eradicate poverty and a better life for all."
– Nelson Mandela

Table of Contents

To

My New Sisters in Christ,

God Bless You for

showing so much kindness

toward me.

In Christ Love,

Glendyn Keeter

May 22, 2014

Acknowledgements

Family members, many friends and professionals made an influence and contribution to my life and to this book. I want to acknowledge them with love and gratitude:

To my parents who gave me life and taught me from the very beginning of my childhood that God is the most important focus in life.

To my beloved brother Norman who took care of my sisters Lynette, Rosemary and me. Norman inspired me to write this book. His contribution to this book and to my life continues to be incalculable. Thank you to my dear sisters for being in my life.

To my dear late Aunty Pete and late Uncle John: thank you for your love, enormous support and for teaching me from the age of ten that education is the road to success. I would like to express my appreciation to my Uncle John who provided me with information on my father whom I did not know on a personal level.

A sincere acknowledgement to my cousins Victor and Lurline Kester who gave their time, guidance and support toward my siblings and my self. Thank you.

To my godfather, Professor Ralph Kester, who expressed that he loved me which was so precious to me.

To the late Nan Timmins, my mother Marguerite, Janine, Jennifer, Graham and Cassondra thank you for being in my life. Your support and love will be remembered.

Thank you to my ex-spouse for teaching me about life.

To the Salvation Army Officers and staff at the Salvation Army Evangeline Residence in Toronto who rescued me from a parent who did not know any better. Thank you for opening up a big door.

A special recognition to Pastor David Payne of The Campus Church, thank you and God bless you, sir, for your extreme kindness, generosity and words of encouragement. To Pastor Phil McConnell, Pastor Stephen, Bonnie and Barry, Gabriela and Juergen, Alison and Peter of Community Bible Church (The Campus) who taught me about Christ, forgiveness, life and family.

Your outpouring of love will always be remembered as you often prayed, advised, and counselled me through my countless trials and tribulations. Thank you all for helping me discover my way.

To my four Christian therapists; thank you for your benevolence and wise counsel.

To my dear friends Lavina, Taye, Sandy, Bonnie, Jackie, Jenny, Lori, Laura, and Dorothy; thank you for your devotion and for not giving up on me.

Finally, to my Lord and personal Saviour, thank you for saving me from a lifetime of severe mental anguish and who spoke and made His existence known to me in my darkest hours.

Introduction

My father died in the summer of June 1993. I did not know how to feel about his death. I had not been permitted to show any emotion or express my feelings during all the years I had lived with him. No tears were ever shed at home.

My brother summoned us to the hospital where my father's lifeless body lay. My father's big brown eyes were still wide open. Uncle John arrived at the hospital and gazed upon my father's body in grief and closed my father's eyes. He placed his hand on my father's forehead and said a silent prayer over my father. I remember saying, "Now you are at peace, Dad." My brother wanted me to hold my father's hand but I was still frightened of him, even in death.

At the funeral I tried to cry. But I was incapable of shedding tears over his passing. My healing and forgiveness came years later. My father's house was either *one of complete silence* or *one of rage.* I had no voice during all those painful

GLENDYN KESTER

years living with my father. There was no communication at home. I felt I had no value and that I was not good enough until one day, *God touched my life*.

South Africa: "Home"

CHAPTER 1

"Let your light shine upon others so that they will fall in your footsteps."

-Nelson Mandela

My father was the youngest of seven children. At fifteen years of age my father falsified his age by declaring himself a year older and enlisted in the Union Defence Force (UDF). In 1941, after three months of training in Pretoria, my father was sent to North Africa as a member of the Eighth Army. He was made a corporal and earned a stripe in the field army as a Sergeant. When he was in Cairo, he played in a weekend rugby tournament for South Africa against Britain, Australia and New Zealand, and ended up winning the tournament. After spending three years in the UDF, in 1944 he was transferred to Mossel Bay in South Africa where he was responsible for demobilizing hundreds of soldiers returning from war. After three months, my father had had enough of the war and he obtained his discharge from the army. He returned to Kimberley with a bicycle and medals for his service.

My father's parents wanted him to further his studies at the university level to become a medical doctor, but he disappointed them. Instead, he obtained a job making up orders at a wholesale firm called Awerbuck and Browne on Transvaal Road in Kimberley. My father told his parents and his brother he had seen too much blood in the war and was adamant about not going to medical school. He worked for several years at Awerbuck and Browne while living at home with his parents and assisted them tremendously by supplementing his father's meagre income as a garbage truck driver.

In 1948, my father and two of his friends travelled throughout the Northern Cape from Vryburg to Upington, registering voters by the dozens. Sir Harry Oppenheimer won the election and received a huge majority largely due to the efforts put forth by my father and his two friends. Mr. Oppenheimer wanted to compensate my father and his friends for their efforts, but instead they asked for employment in the De Beers Diamond Mining Company, of which Mr. Oppenheimer was the Chairman. My father and his friend Sonny were appointed Commissioners of Oaths (C.O.) mainly because they had to swear in the men they registered as voters and also sign the confessions of offenders. My father found himself increasingly busy filling in pension application forms for many old-aged people who did not know they were entitled to a pension.

My father was the leading official of more than fourteen welfare organizations, along with being the Chairman of Transvaal Road Primary School, the Thistles Rugby Club, the Beaconsfield Wanderers Cricket Club, and the Auditor of the South African Rugby Union. During his later years in Kimberley, he served on several school committees where he played a prominent role in educational discussions, the appointment of teachers, and laying down educational policies. My father also raised a tremendous amount of funds for the school where his brother John was the principal.

My father and his friend started the B.E.S.L. (British Empire Service League) with his friend as Chairman and my father as Secretary, a position he held for eleven years, seeing to the needs of the soldiers returning from the war. My father was an extremely valuable asset to the community of Kimberley, especially for the part he played in matters of education, in the social advancement of the people, and in considering the needs of the returning soldiers of WWII. He voluntarily and freely gave of his time and labour to build the Anglican Church of Saint Barnabas, Florianville in Kimberley. This saved the church authorities thousands of pounds in building expenses, as mentioned by the Bishop.

Our Way of Life

"Train a child in the way he should go, and when he is old he will not turn from it."

Proverbs 22:6

In 1954, my father met my beautiful mother Blanche following an after-match reception held at the Hotel Kemo. The Transvaal Women's Hockey Team, my mother's team, was playing against Griqualand West. After the field hockey encounter, my father visited my mother in "Joburg" (Johannesburg – "the City of Gold") for a year or so, and then they were married.

One by one, the four of us children were born in the city of Kimberley, known for its diamonds, in the country of South Africa. As a family man, my father was devoted to his children but he was extremely busy with "outside affairs." He left the upbringing and training of us children to my mother. In that generation it was extremely important for the husband to provide for his family. My mother was a stay-at-home mom. She would discipline us with a leather strap my father made, which he named after an ice cream called "cherry top." We would be asked if we wanted the "cherry top" when we misbehaved. I earned that strap for being a naughty little girl. However, when my mother could not control the four of us children, she would say to us, "Wait until your father comes home."

My parents were very strict with us about minding our manners. In that generation, *children were meant to be seen and not heard.* We were told to have *respect for our elders.* This was very important to my parents, and in South Africa, children had to listen to their parents. We were expected to call any older woman *"Auntie."* That was our custom.

Sundays were a day for attending church and a time set aside for family. Every business was closed. On this very holy day, my mother would take us children to the Anglican Church, and at night taught us how to get down on our knees and say our prayers. I saw my mother as a woman of God. She taught us according to the Bible. She spent a lot of time dressing us up for church. My sisters and I wore beautiful dresses, little white lace gloves, carried pink little purses and wore our hair in long curls. My baby brother had to wear a suit with shiny black polished shoes. Dressing up for church was normal in our culture. After returning from church, we changed out of our church attire and into our everyday clothes. My mother was quite gifted. In her spare time she would sew dresses for us girls on her old fashioned antique sewing machine. She also enjoyed making exquisite embroidered table cloths with napkins to match.

Many women wore beautiful hats to church and other events because the sun was very hot in South Africa. The seasons are reversed in South Africa. When it is wintertime here in Canada, it is summertime in South Africa. Temperatures reach over one hundred degrees in the summer, and in those days, air conditioning was unheard of. In the wintertime there is no heat in people's houses, even to this day. My cousin Lindwill told me that one becomes accustomed to the cold in the winter months.

We had three servants working for us. One woman was hired to do the laundry. She was a Zulu woman who smoked a pipe and washed our clothes by scrubbing them with her hands on a big flat wooden board in a big zinc tub of water using a bar of soap. The wet clothes were hung on an outside clothes line.

Mariah was another servant who cleaned our house. My mother was very particular that the house appeared immaculate. The floors had to be polished and my mother had to see the shine on them. I liked Mariah as she brought her little baby to work sometimes and let her baby sleep on the ground underneath our big lemon tree in our backyard while she performed her duties. As a little girl, there were times I held and played with her little baby, thinking it was a doll.

Marcus was the third servant, and he worked as our gardener. Many people in South Africa had huge, beautiful flower gardens and fruit trees in big backyards.

Marcus pruned our fruit trees which was an enormous task. We had a huge grape vine, a very big lemon tree, and a peach tree. Marcus would also take care of the beautiful rose garden in front of our house. As a child, I would climb over our neighbour's fence and steal large ripe peaches from their backyard. I was never caught. I would eat those scrumptious peaches but later paid a hefty price with a very bad stomach ache. We were not rich. Having servants was part of our way of life as South Africans. We lived a very simple life like most people in South Africa. We did not live extravagantly or have many material things in our home. Material things to my parents were not important. God was foremost in our family, according to my mother. My brother, sisters and I did not have many toys to play with. We would each have one toy and sometimes we made our own toys. We made mud houses with the sand, played games, skipped rope, and drew on the sand. We all liked to play with marbles as they were very inexpensive.

My mother was a simple woman but was very beautiful. She did not wear a lot of makeup. She wore beautiful clothes but did not acquire many. She wore her shiny long brown hair down and sometimes in a braid. My mother never painted her nails with nail polish and her nails were always short. She was tall and slender and had a very light coloured complexion. She used to tell us, "You children should be satisfied with what you have."

We had a dog named Bobby which was my oldest sister's dog. Bobby became sick and he had to be put down. Our next family pet was a dog called Bonzo. Bonzo was a fox terrier as far as I can remember.

In the 1950's and 1960's, many people did not have cars because they could not afford them. We walked everywhere. This was not uncommon in those days. My father rode his bicycle to work and as a little girl I tried riding that bicycle. My father caught me one day. I received a scolding for riding it because this was the only means of transportation my father had to his work at the De Beers Diamond Mines.

One day, I was playing with our broom in the yard. My mother told me to place the broom back where it belonged. Instead of walking around the house, I found a short-cut and threw the broom over our tall wooden fence which crashed right through the living room window. When my father came home from work, I received a punishment that I will never forget. I was a very naughty child back then.

We did not own a television. During the 1950's and 1960's, no one even knew what a television looked like in South Africa. My mother would have the radio (wireless) playing sometimes. My mother was strict with us children. When we left food on our plate my mother would scold us by saying, "Do you children know how many poor children are starving in the world?"

School was very strict in South Africa. We had to wear uniforms. Each of us had two uniforms. We wore white blouses with a blazer, a tie, and a tunic with a coloured belt in the colours of green and gold. The belt, which was called a girdle, was made out of some kind of material wrapped around the uniform. I don't understand to this day why it was called a girdle. Each school had their own colours. We wore clean polished black shoes and white socks. We were inspected on our appearance by our teachers every day. My mother braided our long hair and tied gold ribbons at the bottom of the two braids that joined. My brother wore grey trousers, white shirt, a tie, black shoes, and a blazer as well.

Speaking in class was forbidden. We had to raise our hand if we knew the answer. After receiving our test results, for every mistake we made, the girls would receive a thrashing on their knuckles with a ruler and the boys had to bend over to receive a strap. We were expected to know how to spell and do our arithmetic. We had homework to complete after school. We were very high achievers, excelling in sports and performing in musical recitals. I loved playing basketball and field hockey just like my mother when she was young. My mother and her sister played field hockey, competing in tournaments and travelling to various cities.

Christmas was a special time for our family. Every year we would attend the De Beers Diamond Mines Christmas Party where my father was employed. The best moment was waiting for Father Christmas (Santa Claus) to arrive on the train. We would all receive presents from him. At Christmas time we were lucky to receive one present at most. The emphasis of Christmas was on baby Jesus, attending church, visiting family, friends, and our neighbours. We would visit from house to house all day long, eating all kinds of delectable food.

My father played in cricket tournaments and our entire family travelled with him to different regions. I remember the time we travelled to Cape Town near the seashore. The white sand by the salty sea water was breathtaking. We swam in the water and basked in the hot South African sunshine. My sister Rosemary went missing and my parents were frantic. As my parents and relatives searched for her, all of a sudden she came up to us walking hand in hand with a policeman. My parents were relieved. My Uncle John, Aunty Pete, Aunty Milly, and Uncle Charles were with us at the sea shore in Cape Town. They were my father's family. They were all very special to us children and played a tremendous role in our lives. I was not fortunate to know my grandparents because I was a very small child when my grandparents passed away. However, I vaguely remember my mother's father, Grandpa Francke. I remember his white hair and that he had a moustache. I do not remember Granny Francke.

My family and I travelled to Durban, Natal and stayed in a rather quaint high-ceilinged hotel surrounded by impressive ferns and palm trees. The night we arrived at the hotel, my mother told us not to lock the hotel door. She was going to have a bath in the hotel bathroom down the hall. Instead of obeying her, we locked the door and fell asleep. We found out the next morning that a very thin waiter had to smash the window and climb through to unlock the door. My parents were not amused by us children at all.

One day, my oldest sister and I were coming home from school. It was raining fiercely. We decided to take a short-cut home. We came to a small stream but the water was rising and the only way to cross over was to walk through the stream and get wet. I attempted to throw my school case containing all my school books over to the other side, planning to walk through the cold water. However, my throw was not successful and down the stream my school case floated. We eventually caught up with it, wet books and all. We were drenched. My mother and father gave us a good scolding since our school books were worth a great deal of money. The books had to be laid out flat to dry. In South Africa it was customary to cover our text books with brown wrapping paper to protect the covers from getting damaged so that the books could be resold.

I always dreaded Saturday mornings. My mother made my siblings and I line up in single file as we waited to get a dose of medicine - Castor Oil to keep us regular. My mother used to add sugar to it in order to avoid that horrible taste. Yuk!

Breakfast was not my favourite meal as a little girl. When my mother served us a bowl of porridge, I could not stand the taste or the sight of it. My mother was determined to make me eat it and tried to fool me by pouring the porridge in a dessert bowl. But I knew better. I was too smart. I turned up my nose and never ate the porridge. These are the only few good memories that I will always treasure.

As far back as four years of age, I can remember that there was a deep, dark secret in our family. I will never forget the day my father chased me. I did not know what I had done to make my father so angry. I was so *frightened*. I ran inside the house and locked the big wooden back door. My father started banging on the door while screaming. I looked around the house for my mother but could not find her to protect me. *I was just a little girl.* This was the beginning of my nightmare.

Affliction of a Child

"For the creation was subjected to frustration, not by its own choice, but by the will of the one who subjected it, in hope that the creation itself will be liberated from its bondage to decay and brought into the glorious freedom of the children of God."

Romans 8:20-21

Much of my childhood memories of life growing up in South Africa included living with an intense fear of my father. I experienced incredible and enormous pain. The suffering was too extreme for any young child to endure. Yet, it happened to me. I tried for years not to remember the emotional distress that occurred back in South Africa. *I blocked it totally out of my mind for forty years.* My mother kept on leaving us because of the excessive and frequent abuse and violence perpetrated by my father. I did not understand what was happening because I was so young. As a child there were so many nights when I would cover my tiny little ears with my pillow to stop me from hearing the abuse and violence that my poor mother suffered. I was a just a little girl, and I cried too.

In South Africa, I witnessed my mother try to commit suicide several times. On one particular day, a neighbour came running to our house, telling my father that my mother was sitting on the railway tracks with my baby brother in her arms waiting for the train to come. I was a witness to this as a young five year old. My mother's life was one of much misery for almost twenty years. My father continued to abuse my mother in unimaginable ways. As a little girl, there were many days where I stood in our big kitchen and saw my parents fighting. My mother told my father she was going to tell the neighbours about the abuse. He told her if she did that he would have her "committed." I did not understand what that meant.

One day, my mother showed me her hugely battered and bruised body. The father who I looked up to as a man was supposed to love my mother, not hurt her. The *trust between a father and his little girl was immediately broken.* I suppose this was one way of my mother wanting me to tell someone, *anyone*, by showing me her bruised body. My mother was very religious. When my father finished beating my mother she would send me to the neighbour's house who was a Catholic and my mother would ask for the neighbour to bless the water. It was a cry for help on my mother's part. My mother would ask the neighbours and our relatives to pray for her. I was only a little girl. I did not understand. She could not endure the torture of the abuse and violence in our home anymore.

My memories of my childhood in South Africa and Canada are horrible, as one friend put it, "You only hear of this happening in the movies, Glendyn." The events that took place in our home were like what you would see in a violent horror movie. It was so frightening for any little child to experience. Yet, this happened to me, my poor mother and my siblings.

On Sundays for lunch my mother took great pride in preparing the main meal of the day for our family. One Sunday after church, my father went on a rampage again. My mother took all of us children and ran to an old friend's house who she frequently visited. I was just five years old and my mother screamed, "Glendyn, grab the nappies on the clothes line." These were cloth diapers hanging on the outside clothes line. We ran to a neighbour's house for safety.

At night I could not bear to hear the cruel noises coming from my parent's bedroom. Their bedroom was beside mine. My father's cursing offended my tiny innocent ears then and even today. Suddenly, my mother disappeared one day. I was 9 years old. We had a nanny by the name of Mrs. Barlow, who cared for us children while my father went to work. *That was the last time I saw my mother for almost eighteen years.*

Canada

CHAPTER 4

"When bad things happen to a good person,
God seems distant and silent."

JOB - Introduction

More shocking news came in 1969. My father announced that we were leaving for Canada *without my mother*. I was 10 years old. Upon hearing this devastating news, my young lonely heart ached for my dear mother. Because I was so young, I did not understand why my mother could not come with us to Canada. My father went to Canada first. We stayed at our neighbour's house before following my father to Canada. Before we moved, my sister wrote to my father in Canada asking him why my mother could not come with us. My father wrote back briefly explaining that my mother was sick and that she could not be with us. That was all that was said.

When it came time for my siblings and I to fly to Canada to live with my father, my father instructed a close friend who drove us from Kimberley to Jan Smuts Airport in Johannesburg to not let my mother come close to us children. My mother was not allowed to say good-bye to us. I found this out when I became a young woman. For many years I could not understand why my mother abandoned us and never came to see us off at the airport before we immigrated to Canada. The abandonment through the years caused emotional scars as we had been left motherless.

On our flight to Canada the stewardesses on the airplane looked after us. My baby brother was being naughty on the plane kicking a passenger's seat. So, we all had to move to the back of the airplane. The stewardess gave us boxes of animal-shaped cookies. This kept us happy for awhile. It was our first time being on an airplane. I do not remember anything else or how I felt being on this big airplane. We stopped over in England first before continuing on our journey to Canada. It was an incredibly long journey to Canada - over twenty hours - because it was halfway around the world. In England was the first time I saw television. I was very curious sitting on the floor looking in absolute wonder and awe at this box with cartoons playing on it.

It was winter in 1969 when we finally arrived in Canada. Uncle John picked us up at the airport. The first thing that caught my eye was people driving on the wrong side of the road. I asked Uncle John about it. He explained to me that in Canada everyone drove on the opposite side to South Africa. We were taken to Uncle John and Aunty Pete's house to stay.

Life at Uncle John and Aunty Pete's house was good for awhile but then *evil* came back. Once we were settled in Canada my father started to physically, mentally, and emotionally abuse me and my siblings. One day, my cousin made chocolate muffins for the church youth group. I eyed those muffins and stole one which only left eleven. My sisters, brother and I were all punished until someone confessed. We were not allowed to watch television for a whole week. This was shear torture because I loved watching television which was a luxury since it was something new to me. Finally, I confessed. My father waited until no one was home at Aunty Pete and Uncle John's house. He screamed, at me and physically abused me. I went rolling down the steep basement staircase. *I was just a little girl.* I told no one. This was the beginning of my battered life.

Living at my Aunty Pete and Uncle John's was very lovely and so special to me. Both Aunt Pete and Uncle John instilled in me that education was very important for one to succeed in life. One day while I was helping Aunty Pete in her beautiful rose garden, my Uncle John came up to me and said, "Glendyn, how many books have you read?" It was our first summer holiday from school in Canada. I looked up at my Uncle John with a frown because I had read none. Little did he know that Aunty Pete was teaching me the many different names of roses in her gardening books.

Our first summer in Canada was a lot of fun because Uncle John took us children to the Canadian National Exhibition. Uncle John gave my siblings and me five dollars each. We went on the different children's rides and Uncle John bought us candy floss and treats.

Aunty Pete and Uncle John took us to the Anglican Church every Sunday. My oldest sister and I joined the youth group. We were fortunate to go to summer camp with the youth one weekend. We received tremendous trouble from the camp leaders as the boys sneaked into the girl's dormitory. Camp was exciting and so were Friday evenings at church where we gathered with the other youth at the church to be taught about God. We were given small personal Bibles and we were told to write our name and address in these Bibles. I did not know that God was *pursuing* me from this day forward.

September arrived and school was fun. I was happy meeting new friends. I was at school in my classroom when the first snow fell. I was so excited. I ran to the window in our classroom when I first saw these white flakes falling from the sky. I stuck my nose to the window in amazement. I started jumping up and down. My teacher and the other students were very amused at me.

At lunch time we would run home for lunch to Aunty Pete's house when we were still living there. I loved my Aunty Pete's peanut butter sandwiches and steaming hot Campbell's soup that she fed us on very cold winter days. Aunty Pete was very loving and caring to me and my siblings. She made life easier for us children in the absence of my mother.

One day, I overheard my father ask Aunty Pete if she could take care of us children while he found an apartment for himself. I did not know what was said after that. The very *sad* day came when we had to move out on our own with my father.

However, we still spent time at Uncle John and Aunty Pete's home during the holidays. The parties at Uncle John's and Aunty Pete's house were the best with South African music playing. The aroma and savoury taste of Aunty Pete's specialty, chicken curry and rice, filled the air. There were many uncles, aunts and cousins doing South African dances. That generation loved to hold parties and could they ever dance!

I fondly remember when my godfather Uncle Ralph and his beautiful wife Aunty Ilse came to visit from England. My godfather would pick me up and swing me around and around. He would give me piggy back rides. My godfather was a professor and a surgeon. Actually, my godfather is my cousin. My parents taught me to call them "aunty" and "uncle" because it showed respect. I still honour my parents' wishes to this day. Later on in my fifties, my godfather told me he loved me and he hugged me. This was so very precious to me; something my own father could not convey to me.

At Christmas, my Aunty Pete would always make her famous Christmas pudding which included putting dimes and nickels in it. It was a lot of fun to see who would get the most money. This was a South African tradition. My mother used the same recipe. The kindness and love that Aunty Pete and Uncle John showed us children will never be forgotten. These are the most precious memories that I will always cherish.

A LETTER TO MY MOTHER

202 Wellesworth Drive
Etobicoke, Ontario
Toronto, Canada

March 9, 1970

Dear Mummy,

How is mummy keeping? We are all in good health. Thank you for the money and the necklace which you sent me.

Aunty Milly gave us a necklace too. The schools are closing on the 20th of March, 1970. We are missing mummy a lot.

I am sorry to end my letter so quickly.

Your loving daughter,
Glendyn
Age: 10 years old

Life in the Apartment

"From birth I was cast upon you; from my mother's womb you have been my God. Do not be far from me, for trouble is near and there is no one to help"
Psalm 22:10-11

The year was 1970. The apartment was our new home now. My father provided us with the basic necessities of life which was a roof over our heads, food and a little clothing. We were living in complete poverty. My father was a very hard worker as he tried to provide for us children.

After coming home from work he would spend a lot of time reading the newspaper each day and watching the news, sports and old black and white movies on television. My father would not sit with us at the dinner table at home. He ate his meals sitting in front of the television. This went on for years. As a young child and teenager, I could not understand why my father would not sit with us or talk to us children. I felt worthless after so much rejection, neglect and abandonment. I missed my mother terribly. Words cannot express the grave *loss* I often felt of being *motherless*.

My heart and my spirit were in pieces. I was very broken. The despair that was inflicted upon us by my father was more than we could bear as young children. *My father used fear to control us.* I often felt unloved and had such a sense of hopelessness. I felt of no value to him. My life was a shattered mess. I started putting up walls and went into a fantasy world to protect myself. I would not let anyone come close to me.

We were abused physically, emotionally and mentally by my father. Calling the police or telling anyone what was taking place in our home was not an option; it was our *secret*. I am sure the teachers in our schools suspected. But in those days back in the early 1970's, the laws against abuse and violence against innocent children were kept in the closet. We were all underage. It was my wish for *someone, anyone* to put an end to this drawn-out pain. I feared for our lives. My father became an alcoholic in his later years.

I was terribly frightened of my father. I did not feel safe. Our life with my father was either *one of complete silence* or *one of rage* and this is how we lived for years with no communication at all. *We told no one.* The silence was dreadful. My siblings and I lived in constant fear. It was unbearable. These conditions caused me to become very lonely and fearful. I had much anxiety and I worried constantly. Through my eyes, the world I viewed as a child seemed very frightening. I developed an extreme lack of confidence and very poor self-esteem. I turned my anger inward and I developed major depression in my teenage years with an extreme lack of motivation.

It was difficult for me to concentrate on my schooling. The loneliness and fearing for our lives as children was unthinkable to speak of. I never looked forward to the holidays because it meant that my father was home. I grew into a quiet, passive, very lonely, timid teenager. As a young woman, I suppressed my feelings and showed no emotions for years.

I just barely passed high school. I dropped several important subjects. A teacher told me one day. "Glendyn, you are going to need this major course in life." But, I dropped it anyways. I was only a teenager. I did not know any better. I struggled with school and found it quite difficult because I had the trauma at home to deal with. My father never became involved with our studies or schooling. There was no nurturing, love or guidance in our home. The strong desire to be with my mother was too painful to describe. We were born and thrown out into the world to *fend* for ourselves. We were taught no life skills or much of anything. When my father was in the living room, my siblings and I were in the other parts of the townhouse, making sure we did not make a sound to make him angry. I felt like a very lost soul. I did not fit in anywhere or belong anywhere.

My oldest sister was put in charge to take the place of my mother and to raise my siblings and me. It was a South African custom to put the eldest in charge of the younger children. My sister did her very best even though she was only thirteen years of age. She cooked the meals, cleaned the home, did the laundry and helped my father with the groceries. She accomplished these chores without complaint. She had the caring and loving nature that my mother had for us children. This was an incredible responsibility for her. I, on the other hand, dreaded these chores, especially because of the way we were treated by my father. But in the end, I helped my sister.

We met friends in our apartment building and went to school. We only stayed at the apartment for a short time and then we moved to a townhouse in Rexdale, Ontario. It was difficult to move again and leave our friends.

My siblings and I could not wait for Saturday evenings to come because my father would always go out and come home very late, or in some cases, not at all for the weekend. We would turn the music up loud and start dancing in our apartment and the townhouse. This was like heaven to us, feeling *free* and *safe* because it was a *happy* time even if it was just for a little while.

My Only Hope, Reaching Out to God

"Help me, O Lord my God; save me in accordance with your love. Let them know that it is your hand, that you, O Lord, have done it. They may curse, but you will bless; when they attack they will be put to shame, but your servant will rejoice."

Psalm 109:26-28

The first time I opened up and talked about our dark *secret* life was in 2002 to my cousin Victor and his wife, Lurline. They could not bear to hear about this because it was a complete shock to them. They were *horrified*. My father treated everybody else's children better than his very own. As the years went on, I felt *I was not good enough*. I yearned for my father's approval and acceptance.

One day, my sister and I invited some boys into our townhouse. My father came home. The boys ran out the back door and jumped over the fence. My father rushed after them and screamed, "Do you think I am some kind of monster? I have a big gun you know."

In 1973, when I was 14 years old and in grade nine, I began to frequent the bars and night club scene in downtown Toronto. My oldest sister met a girl at high school who led us into the night life in Toronto. I did not realize the bad choices that I was making. I only saw it as an *escape* from an unsafe home life. My oldest sister was 16 years old. This girl showed us how to change our identification high school card to make us appear older in order to enter the night clubs. We went to these bars every weekend and sometimes on a week night as well. There were times that I would go alone. We would dance the night away.

However, I did not know the danger that was ahead of me. We did not get ourselves into any kind of trouble with the law. In the 1970's we attended the Yonge Street Mall in Toronto where part of the street was closed off. Many people from all over came to this outdoor mall and at night we would go bar hopping. One night, I met a man at one of these night clubs who was older than me. This man lured and seduced me. He took away my innocence at the age of 15. He first physically assaulted and then raped me because I said *no* to him for not wanting to have sex with him. He sexually abused me repeatedly for one year. He kept on pursuing me. I did not know any better. I was so naïve and innocent.

I found out later that he was a repeat offender when the police came to our door. The police wanted me to testify against him in court. He was a pimp and I was given strong advice to stay away from him by the police. My father and my siblings knew nothing about this incident. I was subpoenaed to testify in court. It hurt terribly but the policeman made me realize that this man was no good for me. I stopped seeing him. I mailed a thank you card to that policeman later. Due to what happened because of the rape and sexual abuse, I developed a sexual addiction and a problem with lust which I discovered through Christian therapy in the year 2000. However, the sexual addiction started much younger because of the feeling of rejection towards me by my father. I was so ashamed of this that I sought further therapy on and off. Most importantly I cried out to God for help to take this from me. I can truthfully say today I am victorious and free from this wicked sin.

My lonely and young heart ached for my dear mother. I blocked that whole year with this man out of my mind for thirty eight years until the memories surfaced when I was 53 years old. I just kept on living my life with my father and my siblings. I prayed for my mother, father, siblings and everyone in the world as my dear mother taught me. I said this prayer every night for many years.

In grade nine, I started working as a part-time waitress at a restaurant. I stayed there for one year. Someone told me at the restaurant, "Hey Glendyn, I know of a place that is hiring and they pay more." I applied for the job and I was hired immediately as a part time sales clerk at the Jane and Finch Mall. I worked very hard some evenings during the week and every weekend while completing my high school and on into my college years. I stayed at the store for five years. I bought some furniture for our home to help my father because it was difficult on his meagre income to purchase any "extras." When not working or attending school, my oldest sister and I had chores to perform at home. I had to sew my father's torn clothes and iron his suits for work. The girls were not allowed to stay after school for any extra-curricular activities. I was quite good at long jump, gymnastics and basketball, but I was unable to compete because I had to be at home.

I always felt like an unwanted child. I felt like garbage left by the roadside. Feeling I had no voice, I became the victim of extreme childhood abuse and so did my siblings. I felt a lot of shame and guilt. I became very insecure.

One day, my father screamed at me, "You are good for nothing!" This left tremendous emotional scars on me. These horrible words stuck in my mind over the years. I left home when I was 17 years old. My father drove me with my suit case to a group home which a Guidance Counsellor at school found for me after telling her of the unsafe conditions at home.

During my stay at the group home, I went for a few counselling sessions with a psychiatrist at the Lakeshore Psychiatric Hospital. It was my first time seeing a psychiatrist. The psychiatrist asked me, "Can I record you so that you can hear how you sound when you talk about your mother?" I replied, "Yes." My voice sounded so *soft* as I lowered my voice every time I spoke about my mother. I would also get a tremendous headache. It was too painful for me to talk about her. I only saw the psychiatrist for a few sessions. I lived in the group home with other teenage girls who were also fleeing from abusive homes. I graduated from high school while still working part-time. I rented an apartment with a friend from the group home. Things did not work out with my friend. Unfortunately, I returned to my father's home.

One day, I looked out the window when I was 19 years old. I thought to myself, "There must be more to life than this, and if this is what a family is all about I am not going to have a family." I felt like a prisoner. I did not realize that *I was a prisoner within myself.* I started buying household items and hid them in my closet to give me the assurance that I was going to leave for good again. But, I stayed. I cried in those quiet moments by myself when I thought of what my life had become.

I felt *hopeless.* I did not trust *anyone.* The longing to be with my mother was indefinable. I cried myself to sleep so many nights. My pillow would be soaking wet from the many tears that I shed. I imagined that I was back in my mother's loving arms feeling safe and loved as I embraced my pillow at nights.

When my father was in his rages I would cry out to God in desperation at night in my prayers. I would plead with God saying, *"God, please make me a better person to help other people."* I prayed this prayer for years. But, I strayed away from God. In fact, I think I was very angry with God for making me suffer through this horrific life that seemed to have *no end* to it.

At home we were never allowed to speak of my mother. As I grew up, I realized that was because of the stigma attached to my mother having a mental illness. In my father's generation, mental illness was kept in the closet and it was taboo to speak of it. The stigma is still very much alive today and many people do not want to talk about it. I blocked my mother and my memories of her out of my mind for years. My mother suffered dearly and I don't think she ever knew the *danger* her poor children were in.

A Cry of a Child

"O God, hear my prayer, listen to my plea; Strangers are attacking me; violent men are trying to kill me. They have no regard for God."

Psalm 54:2-3

My last year of college was extremely challenging. My father always complained to my oldest sister that I was not doing any chores at home. I was extremely busy trying to complete my college assignments. My father did not understand. I was determined and as difficult as it was, I wanted to succeed and make something of myself. Living with my father was like walking on egg shells all of the time. I wanted out.

One day, my father tried to strangle me. He screamed at me saying, *"Now we will finish it. We can kill each other."* I was 17 years old. I did not understand what I did that was so bad that my father would want me dead. I thought there must be something wrong with me. I thought everything was my fault. I thought that I was the reason for the break up of my parent's marriage as well.

Later in life it became very difficult for me to handle life's issues and problems that arose. I had a difficult time making decisions because we had not been prepared for the outside world. I started to escape into a fantasy world when I was at home. I would fantasize that my godfather would come and take me away to England so that my father would not hurt me anymore or that I would meet someone and get married then I would not live through this nightmare anymore.

When we were at home, we would all watch television along with my father sitting in the living room. We sat there *very quietly*. We did not *dare* move or make a sound. We did not talk or laugh even when something was funny on the television. *We never laughed.* We were like *dummies.* This was completely unnatural. When not watching television we would be in our bedrooms just lying on the bed reading or staring into space saying nothing. Even though we were siblings, we did not know how to relate to each other or other people. I would try to read and complete my homework at home but it became increasingly difficult because one of my siblings was diagnosed with Schizophrenia. It was also very challenging for me because I was trying to protect her from my father.

I almost gave up college because of my emotional struggles. When my father came through the front door, my siblings and I would run to our bedrooms because the less we saw of him the *safer* we felt. One Sunday morning my father began watching a church service on television. I wondered if he was trying to make peace with God. All of a sudden he screamed, "You children need to go to church!" But we did not go.

When my father brought one of his girlfriends home, my sister and I were *ordered* to prepare dinner for her, and then clean up all the dirty pots and dishes after. I felt like Cinderella. We were *only* children and still in high school. One day during my college years, I stood up to my father. I walked out when he invited many people over for dinner.

As I grew into a young woman, I harboured great hatred, anger, bitterness and resentment toward my father. I was kept in emotional bondage for 40 years. I was unable to experience the joy that God planned for my life. I could not move forward in life. I spent less time at home. I stayed at college because I did not want to go home. I kept myself extremely busy by picking up an extra evening course while still attending college full-time. I was still working part-time because I had to put myself through college for my first year. I desperately wanted to succeed in life. I spent some time dancing in disco clubs which helped me to forget my troubles, even if only for a short time. I even dated a few boys. I knew nothing of relationships. In the end, the relationships were short and did not survive. I was confused about what love was but I longed for someone to love me.

One of my siblings ended up in an insane asylum in Toronto. The way this place operated back in the 1970's must haunt her for life. My sister could not endure the mistreatment from my father any longer. My father did not want to give her an allowance, so she ran away from home and ended up on the street. My sister ended up in trouble with the law because she was hungry.

I was forced to go to court with my father. I noticed that my sister's shoes were all tattered and torn. This was in the wintertime. I was heartbroken for her. I felt so sorry for her that I went out and bought her new boots. Life was extremely difficult for my siblings and me. On top of everything else, my father became an alcoholic in his later years.

One day, I sensed something was not right with me. My friend from college asked me, "Did you take a shower?" I lied and said, "Yes." She said, "You did not." Shocked and embarrassed, shame overcame me. My hygiene had never been a problem. When I arrived home, I jumped into the shower. I started to cry, but ignored what I was feeling. I was keeping secrets from my friends and everyone. I felt isolated. The loneliness was unbearable.

Thinking back, some of my teachers knew something was wrong with me. But nobody reached out to me except for one teacher toward the very end of my last semester. He sent me to the president's administrator of the college – a friend he knew personally. She provided me with a small room in which to complete my assignments and also assisted me with a bursary. This helped in my schooling, but it did not help me with my secrets.

She then sent me to the college counsellor and that is when I opened up a little. She must have felt so sorry for me because she hugged me. Hugging was very *foreign* to me. My father never once hugged us. I left the counsellor's office rather quickly. As I opened the door to leave she asked me, "Will you come back Glendyn?" I said, "I don't know." When I went back the counsellor arranged for me to see a psychiatrist. When the psychiatrist called I refused to see him. I even tried to live in a shelter in downtown Toronto, but the shelter was so dirty inside that home seemed more like a palace. I called a public health nurse and she came to our home. *I was desperate.* But, my father walked in. He told the nurse that I was just fine. The nurse left her business card.

My Wounded Psyche

"A man reaps what he sows to please his sinful nature, from that nature will reap destruction; the one who sows to please the Spirit, from the Spirit will real eternal life."

Galatians 6:7-8

In 1980, I finally graduated from college in Travel and Tourism after two years of working very diligently for this diploma. My father and my oldest sister attended my graduation. I was 21 years old. I tried looking for a full time job that summer but my father wanted me home to perform all the household chores. I became very confused about what role I was supposed to play in our family. One night, something was horribly wrong with me. I woke up startled by a pounding feeling in my head. I woke my father up immediately. I said, "Daddy, I need to go to the hospital." My father said, "I will take you to the hospital in the morning." I went back to bed. But I returned to my father's bedroom. I demanded that he drive me immediately to the hospital.

I met with the psychiatrist at the hospital in the emergency ward. I told him briefly of the living conditions at home. My father spoke to the psychiatrist alone. I can only imagine what my father told this doctor concerning my mother. He was very bitter toward my mother. He felt that she was to blame for us children's mental illness. This all had to do with the stigma of mental illness. Mental illness was kept in the closet in those days and still is very much today. *The stigma is worse than having the illness itself.* Mental illness is a disease of the brain and is no fault of the person. I am a person first. I am a human being.

I began living at my aunt and uncle's house again. The psychiatrist at the Emergency ward told my father I needed to go away for awhile someplace quiet. I was put on medication. My Uncle John and my Aunty Pete took me in. Once I was in their home I saw this opportunity as my *escape*. I told my Uncle John that I was not going back home. My Uncle John said I could stay until I was financially sound and able to find a place of my own. I was so happy. I felt safe. But, my Uncle John said, this would cause a strain in his relationship with my father.

I was still working part-time, but I had a meltdown at work. I was not well and became worse. Things only escalated. My thoughts were not normal. I was hospitalized. I thought this could never happen to me. But, I was diagnosed and labelled with having Schizophrenia, just like my sister. *All three of my siblings and I ended up on the mental health ward at the same hospital at different times because of my father.*

During my first few days at the hospital, different nurses kept on over-medicating me to the point that I began to choke. My body stiffened. I managed to drag myself down the hall of the hospital and grabbed onto a nurse. This nurse was tiny and as I found out later, her name was Annie. I held onto Annie for dear life. She coaxed me back to my room. If Annie had not been there at that moment, I would definitely not be alive today. Many nurses ran into my room. I was given an injection and the choking stopped within a few seconds. The stiffening in my feet and body subsided.

I was so very frightened. I signed myself out of the hospital. I ran away from the hospital and stayed with a friend. My family doctor encouraged me to return to the hospital. I went back to my Aunty Pete's and Uncle John's house. But, I became worse. I stopped eating and became very weak due to losing so much weight. My thoughts were not normal. My Aunty Pete took me back to the hospital in a taxi. I painted my face with big circles using red lip stick. The psychiatrist at the hospital asked me, *"Is that your war paint on your face?"* I said, *"Yes."* When I was on the ward I thought to myself I might as well enjoy the ride. I gave the staff one heck of a performance. I became very difficult to handle for the nurses and the psychiatrists because of my father. My father *terrorized* our whole household. The extent of all the violence in our home beginning in South Africa until I reached 21 years old in Canada finally took its toll on me.

I was fortunate that I had managed to graduate from college with high marks. The doctors or nurses did not know that I was severely burnt out completing college, working at my part-time job, taking an extra night school course, trying to live with the trauma at home, looking after my sick sister, plus trying to do some household chores. I always took on excessive work. I just kept on striving so very hard to succeed. I was driven to succeed in life.

I remember one morning while in the hospital I collapsed to the floor. I cried and wailed in a baby's voice. While on the floor I curled up in a *fetal* position as if I was back in my mother's womb. I needed to feel *safe*. I needed *protection*. I had a huge hole missing in my heart for Mother. As I lay on the floor in the hospital I felt a hand stroking me gently and even though I was in such a fragile frame of mind, I heard a voice say, *"It is alright."* *"It is alright, there."* It was one of the psychiatrists who comforted me. My brother told me later that I behaved like a very little girl when he visited me. *I was 21 years old.* I lost so much weight. I was given huge bottles of Ensure to drink to add weight onto my small thin body. My father visited me twice while I was in the hospital. It was very uncomfortable and frightening for me to be with him. He did not talk much.

I was uncontrollable and naughty at the hospital. I was put in restraints. I did not like the restraints at all. At night both my hands and feet were strapped to the bed, and in the morning I was taken out of the restraints. *However, I knew better.* When the nurse came to put me into the restraints at night I already managed to put myself in them. In the morning I would already be out of the locked restraints. The nurses and my psychiatrist could not figure out how I did this. Another time I was confined to my hospital room. I was being mischievous. I ran down the hospital hall stark naked. To my surprise, I bumped right into my psychiatrist! He received the biggest shock of his life. My psychiatrist and another nurse each grabbed me under an arm. They picked me up, dragging me back to my hospital room. I went back kicking and screaming. I guess I was being the little girl that I never had a chance to be.

One day, I needed to use the bathroom but I was unable to get out of the restraints. Now the hospital staff made the restraints tighter. I pressed the call bell and the nurse let me out to go to the bathroom. But I was unable to go. When I really had to use the bathroom again, the nurses would not let me out of the restraints. They thought I was being mischievous. They would not answer my call bell again. I was forced to use my hospital bed as a washroom. When morning came there was a different nurse on duty. A nurse I never saw before. I called her Grandma because in my mind I thought she really was my grandmother. She took me out of the restraints and cleaned me up. She was not very happy with what she found.

I was sharing a hospital room with other patients and because I was so out of control and disturbed the other patients in the room. I was transferred to a room all to myself. I thought to myself; "Now what could I do to tick the nurses off for putting me in these ghastly restraints again." When the nurse came in she got the shock of her life. Her mouth dropped. I managed to get at least the right hand and right foot out of the restraints. I rearranged all the furniture in the whole room with my free right hand and free right foot!

I told my psychiatrist one day, "My godfather from England is coming to take me away to live with him and his family." My psychiatrist believed this and so did I. But, this was not real. I saw this psychiatrist for eighteen years. He became a father figure to me. At the hospital I refused to take the medication the nurses tried to give me. In my mind, I thought they wanted to poison me. Finally, one male nurse was able to get the medications into me. I became better. When I started to regain my faculties, I began to dress smartly at the hospital. I put on makeup and brushed my long, dark, shiny brown hair. *I pretended to be a nurse and bossed the other patients around. I even reported back to the Charge Nurse.* Visitors coming to visit their loved ones thought that I was really one of the nursing staff. Soon enough they found out that I was a patient. To my disappointment, my brief nursing career was over. To tell you the truth, I do not know how the nurses and the psychiatrists survived with me on that ward. *I was one little devil at that hospital.*

While I was on the ward I met a young man. There was some confusion with our food trays. We received each others tray of food. I never told a soul. Being a mischievous little devil, I mixed up our food trays. He was so angry because his tray had such little food on it. My tray of food had enough on it to feed a horse. This young man looked like a football player. He was *huge*. After he was discharged he came to visit me at the hospital. He brought me one lovely red rose. As I was making good progress in my wellness journey I told my psychiatrist, *"I am not going back home to live with my father."*

I was very frightened to tell my father that I was not going back home. The social worker at the hospital called some group homes and residences. A very kind Christian woman who was a friendly hospital volunteer drove me to various residences and then back to the hospital. When I received passes from the hospital, she took me out to shopping malls where we chatted while sharing a cup of coffee and sometimes a meal. She was my angel sent from God.

The Salvation Army Evangeline Residence

"Jesus said to them, 'Whoever welcomes this little child in my name welcomes me; whoever welcomes me welcomes the one who sent me. For he who is least among you all-he is the greatest.'"

Luke 9:48

The year was 1981. Once I was discharged from the hospital I went to live at the Salvation Army Evangeline Residence in Toronto, a shelter for women only. I was so enthusiastic and appreciative to live in this residence because it looked like a hotel to me. Years later, I found out that it actually used to be a hotel. It was decorated so beautifully with red carpeting throughout the residence. The Salvation Army was the only residence that opened up its doors to welcome and accept me. They came to my rescue just in time.

My life at the residence was sometimes very lonely for me. It had nothing to do with the residence or staff. It was the same loneliness that I had developed as a little girl when I lacked nurturing and love from both of my parents. My self esteem was very low. I became depressed. I stayed in my room. Occasionally, I watched television in the lounge, speaking to the Salvation Army Officers and staff when I was not seeing my boyfriend - the young man from the hospital who brought me the single red rose. I started reading fiction books that a friend from work gave me to read. It was one way of escaping reality to soothe the pain and take away the loneliness.

One of the Salvation Army Officers reminded me of my mother because she was someone who had a gentle loving nature about her. I grew fond of her. The staff at the residence was very caring toward me. I shared a room with another girl and later I was transferred up to the fourth floor. I had a room all to myself. I was on the same floor where some of the Salvation Army Officers lived. You were only asked to live on the fourth floor if you were exceptionally well behaved. At the residence we were encouraged to attend Sunday services in the Chapel. However, I did not attend many and at times I stayed in my room reading Harlequin Romances. I was 22 years old. I did not know that *God's hand was upon my life*. Maybe the loneliness that I had often felt could have been replaced with *God's unconditional love*.

I did not tell anyone at the residence of my troubled past. I behaved myself at the residence always. The staff and the Salvation Army Officers were all very good to me. There were curfews and rules that we had to follow.

Everyone who lived at the residence was not allowed to stay in bed or at the residence all day. You either had to go to school, work, volunteer, or go to a Day Treatment Program at a hospital. I went to a vocational school for the first few months. I looked for a job and I was hired as a full time file clerk. I stayed at this job for almost five years until I found a better paying job.

My boyfriend was my best friend. He took care of me and treated me well. He was very respectful of me. The Salvation Army officers liked him and approved of him. On our first date I wore high heel shoes and a dress. He told me I should change because we were going to Canada's Wonderland. I left my dress on, but I changed the heels and put on flat shoes. When we arrived at Wonderland I did not want to go on any of the rides. I tried to explain to him that I had a weak stomach and did not like heights. He asked, "Well, what did we come here for?" I went on the ride with him. That morning I had a huge breakfast before he came to pick me up. When we got off the ride he noticed that I brought up all over him. My whole breakfast which consisted of two eggs, bacon, homemade fries and toast including two cups of coffee was all over him. I said, "I told you I cannot go on any rides." He went into the washroom quickly and tried to clean up. He came out of the bathroom and we ended up leaving Wonderland immediately. Quite the first date!

I lived at the Salvation Army Residence for a year and a half. The residence was not a permanent home. It was expected that you had to move on. I have never forgotten to this day what a powerful influence the Salvation Army Officers had on my life. The Salvation Army instilled in me that school and employment were very important in life and this is the message that the kind-hearted, compassionate officers left with me to this day.

My Disability

"He answered, John's messengers, 'Go back and tell John what you have seen and heard: the blind can see, the lame can walk, those who suffer from dreaded skin diseases are made clean, the deaf can hear, the dead are raised to life, and the Good News is preached to the poor.'"

Luke 7:22

I moved out from the residence and shared an apartment in downtown Toronto with four other women near Ryerson Technical Institute. It was my first time living independently. I did not like my new home at the apartment. The two things that kept me going were my job and my boyfriend. Some days I would go shopping to buy office clothes for my work and I sure dressed professionally. On rare occasions I went out with my roommates.

In 1982, soon after my move from the Salvation Army Evangeline Residence I found myself pregnant at 22 years of age. It came as a shock to me and my boyfriend because we used protection. I did not have the guidance or mentoring regarding waiting for marriage to have sex. I was left motherless and this was not addressed at home by my abusive father. I already made the decision when I was in my teens and early twenties that I was giving up motherhood due to the strong mental illness and suffering in my family. My boyfriend and I were sent to Sick Children's Hospital in Toronto by my psychiatrist to see a Genetics Doctor. He informed us that our baby would develop serious mental health and psychological problems due to the strong genetics in my family. With the information that was provided by all of my healthcare providers and also because I was having extreme difficulty taking care of myself while suffering with my mental illness, I made the decision to abort the baby. My boyfriend wanted the baby but I did not want any child to go through so much suffering with mental illness and I did not have anyone to help me bring this baby into the world. Later, when I became a mature woman and a Christian I knew that I made a terrible mistake aborting my baby. I went through tremendous grief for the loss of my baby. I was counselled by my mentors through the grieving process. This baby was a life inside me. I killed my baby. I confessed my terrible sin before God.

My father wanted me to return home. But with the little strength I had within me I stayed away. I did not see my father and siblings for a few years, and when I did see my father, which was on a very, very *rare* occasion, I would drag my boyfriend along. I was still so very frightened of my father even though I was now 25 years old. Visiting my father was not very pleasant. My father still controlled me even though I was not living with him. It was difficult for me to look my father in the eyes. I always looked down when I spoke to him. I used to see my father's face everywhere I went. Every old man I saw on the street, on a bus or subway reminded me of my father's face.

I took an evening class at Ryerson University in computers along with a fun dancing class while working full time, even though I did not do well in either class. I continued to see my boyfriend and his family. I saw what life was like in another family where laughter, tears, and expressing one's feelings was all normal. This was not allowed in my father's home.

In 1983 I had a minor relapse. Everything seemed dark and gloomy at home. I did not know at the time that I had sunk into depression. My self esteem was very low. I was barely coping. However, I continued to work full time. I don't know how I survived still working while suffering with depression. My supervisor told me I had to take some time off because he saw that I was not well. My co-workers did not understand what was happening to me when they saw my behaviour. Some were frightened, some were compassionate, and others laughed. I felt extremely embarrassed and ashamed. The shame was unbearable. I knew something was terribly wrong with me. I was frightened. I am not sure how I ended up at the hospital.

When I walked out of the elevator at the hospital I cried, sobbed so loudly that all the nurses came to see me. They remembered me from before. All I heard was, "You did well, Glendyn." I received many visitors including many of the girls from my workplace. I was hospitalized again for a week.

I eventually returned to work after being off for awhile. The first day back at work was extremely difficult and so were the first few months. I felt very ashamed that everyone now knew that I had a mental illness. My supervisor let a co-worker buddy with me for a few months. I was grateful for this *buddy system* which is now called *peer support* today because it made me feel more comfortable at work and my confidence came back. My work had this system in place even back in the early 1980's.

I began dressing very smartly and professionally for the office. My employers were very good to me. I can honestly say that *God touched my life* in such a way that I never went back to that frame of mind *ever* again.

My Wedding Day

"Husbands…be considerate as you live with your wives, and treat them with respect as the weaker partner and as heirs with you of the gracious gift of life, so that nothing will hinder your prayers."

1 Peter 3:7

On September 7, 1985, I was married after a courtship of almost five years. I was 27 years old. I did not know what love or married life was about because of the unstable, unsafe environment of my horrific upbringing. I was very naïve. It was only years later that I learned to love my husband.

I stayed overnight at my Aunty Pete and Uncle John's house before my wedding day. The big day arrived and my cousin's wife Lurline applied my makeup and she assisted me into my wedding gown. It was the hottest and most humid day of the summer. My cousins Victor and Lurline also rented a maroon-coloured limousine as a wedding gift. *I felt so special that day.*

I missed my mother dearly as she was not present at my wedding, but my relatives made it possible for my wedding to be a special day for me. My father wore a white suit with white shoes and walked me down the aisle. My bouquet of flowers that I was holding was shaking terribly. My father said to me, "Look up, Glendyn." I was looking down to the floor still feeling frightened and very nervous.

My Uncle John, Aunty Pete and my cousins played a significant role in helping me with my wedding plans. My father was not pleased with me at first. I did not include him in the wedding plans until he said something to my sister who spoke to me about it. I then went to my father and he helped in the wedding plans. The night at the end of my wedding reception before my new husband and I left, my father said to me. "Glendyn, I want you to be happy." My father kissed me and hugged me. This was the only hug I have ever received from my father. I thanked my father. I was still consumed with fear and still suffering emotionally.

During my marriage, I took my husband along with me to visit my father. The visits were very uncomfortable. My father only said a few words at most and the television was always on. I never understood why my father could not talk to his children and have a conversation with us. Most times my father would lie on the couch and fall asleep during our visits so we would just leave. Later on, I realized that my father was suffering from depression and other psychological problems due to his own upbringing. I invited my father over on occasions when I had company for dinner.

I was not prepared for marriage as I had not received any counselling on marriage or my abuse. My abusive upbringing had an enormous impact on my marriage. Two years after we were married I had an affair which hurt my husband and caused him a lot of pain. I confessed to him and he still wanted to work through our marriage. That is when he took me to church but we never received counseling for the affair. I regretted what I did because the trust that we had for each other was broken. I repented before God in church for the affair with my pastor present. My husband was very good to me and helped me tremendously. Both of us were very hard working and had full time positions. We became very involved in church work. We went travelling and went camping on the Bruce Peninsula. I even learned how to portage with our heavy red painted canoe over the river. I did not like portaging because the canoe was extremely heavy.

I took on a new position that paid more on January 13, 1986 with another insurance company as a data entry clerk. I upgraded my typing skills taking evening courses and practicing at home. I was at this job for seven years. My job was terminated and I did not cope well at home due to my inactivity. I continued my education. I have always enjoyed school.

The "Reunion"

CHAPTER 12

*"My heart is not proud, O Lord, my eyes are not
haughty; I do not concern myself with great matters
or things too wonderful for me. But I have stilled and
quieted my soul like a weaned child with its mother;
like a weaned child is my soul within me."*

Psalm 131:1-2

On November 29, 1986, seventeen years after leaving
South Africa, I returned to South Africa to be
reunited with my mother. My husband and I attended a
South African dance here in Canada the night before my
trip. My father was at the dance. The next day my father
came to see me off at the airport with my husband and my
mother-in-law. My father was trying to change during his
retirement years. My sister said he had mellowed. She and
her little daughter - the only grandchild - spent a lot of
time with my father. My siblings all kept in touch with my
father *except* me. I was still very afraid of my father.

I was going alone to South Africa to meet my mother after almost 20 years being apart from her. The airplane landed in Amsterdam. I did not feel very well because of the late night at the dance. I also did not sleep very well the night before my flight as I was feeling very excited and anxious about my trip. I had a connecting flight to South Africa. My next flight left Amsterdam sixteen hours later. I was too tired to go sightseeing. I went to a day hotel and went to sleep. After sleeping for awhile, I woke up and had a bath which greatly refreshed me.

That night I boarded South African Airways at 11:30 pm. The flight seemed to take forever. We refuelled in Nairobi then flew onto South Africa. As we approached South Africa, I went to freshen up in the bathroom as I was feeling very anxious to see my mother after not seeing her since 1969. I wondered what my mother would look like and what she would think of me. When I went into the bathroom of the airplane it was dark outside and after I came out to sit back down it was as bright as day. It was so beautiful and amazing. In just a few minutes it went from darkness to light. This was one of God's wonderful miracles.

Finally, after the long flight, I arrived in Johannesburg. As I walked through the airport, I found my relatives. I first recognised my aunt and she introduced me to the rest of the family. Then, *I saw my mother.* I did not recognise my mother at all. The sight of my mother was shocking. *She was a total stranger to me.* My heart broke. It was so very painful for me to see what had become of her life. My mother was terribly thin, her hair had turned grey, and she did not look very well at all. She looked so old. The suffering showed on her face tremendously. I remembered her as being so beautiful, alive, and vibrant. But, I forgot that I was a young woman now and the last time I had seen her was when I was 9 years old.

My mother said, *"Hello."* I said, *"Hello Mummy."* I was not sure what to say. My mother did not talk after that. I took my mother's hand. We walked hand in hand. I was taken to one of my cousin's home for dinner after a walk along a lake. I found out that night that my mother was on a three week pass from a hospital, *an insane asylum,* which had been her home for almost twenty years. *My resentment and hatred for my father grew even more.* I was extremely hurt because I had lost my mother. I was still very young and did not know what to say to my mother. I felt that I lost both of my parents a long time ago.

During my stay in South Africa, I had to bathe my mother as she was unable to look after herself. I asked my mother one morning, "Mummy, why did you not see us off at the airport before leaving for Canada?" She told me, *"I was at the airport and I was forbidden to come close to you, Glendyn. It was your father's instructions to his friends who drove you to the airport."* I was speechless. I was so angry at my father. I guess my father feared that maybe my mother would kidnap us. All those years I could not understand why my mother did not come to say goodbye to us before we left for Canada. I thought she just abandoned us.

My mother did not say much to me during my visit at my aunt's place. My reunion with my mother was not a happy one. It was too painful. Nothing was said to me about what happened in those days in the 1950's and 1960's between my parents. Within a week, my mother had to return to the asylum because she became more ill with her mental illness.

One night my cousin took me out. I began to cry. *I wept.* I cried and sobbed my heart out in the back seat of the car as my cousin tried to comfort me. I wanted to go back to Canada, but South Africa represented my *roots.* I felt like I was torn between two worlds. I did not know in my heart where *"home"* was. It was as though I had no home at all.

My mother was supposed to travel with me to different cities in South Africa to visit with my father's family but she was not well enough for the trip. In a way it was a relief to me because it was too traumatic for me to be with her. However, I felt guilty that she was not with me. I wanted to remember my mother the way she was when I was a little girl. She had been a very beautiful woman with an attractive smile and had an air of confidence about her.

Another cousin showed me around and I even received a welcoming message on the South African radio. I travelled alone to Worcester to visit my dad's sister, my Aunt Milly, along with more family. Aunty Milly was also a devoted Christian. She spoiled me terribly. I loved it. In the mornings she placed a teacup and saucer with coffee and homemade baked biscuits on my night table beside my bed before I woke up. Since then, we have corresponded over the years with each other. I met so many of my cousins and aunts that I didn't even know I had. I have a much bigger family than I thought.

Leaving Worcester, I travelled along the coast onto Cape Town and took a bus tour with a friend. While on the bus, baboons were climbing on top of our bus and everyone was taking pictures. These baboons were wild so we had to stay inside the bus. They can be quite dangerous!

As my friend and I walked along the beach, a sand storm hit us. We had to take refuge in a restaurant until the storm passed. I had forgotten that I experienced these storms as a child and how much the sand can hurt your eyes. I swam in the Indian and Atlantic Oceans and I felt in awe at how one ocean can be so warm and the other so cold.

I was captivated by Table Mountain in Cape Town. This was a spectacular sight, a tourist attraction where visitors frequently visited. I was staying at one of my cousin's homes, and as I walked out of the front door of her house I could see Table Mountain right before my eyes. It is such an impressive view.

A week later, I took an airplane to Kimberley, the city I was born in. My father's other brother, Uncle Les, took me on a trip to meet more family. My Uncle Les treated me to ice cream as we chatted on our trip. As we drove along we saw some ostriches. This was the first time I had seen ostriches other than in films and on television. I was captivated by these beautiful animals. I also went on a tour of the Diamond Mines where my father once worked. The "*Big Hole*" was the mine where diamonds were extracted from. This was another tourist site not far from our home in Kimberley.

My last visit was seeing the home that I lived in as a little girl. Seeing the house brought back not only painful memories, but also some of the excitement of my childhood. I took a picture of the house. From my vantage point on the street, I saw the huge grape vine and fruit trees that we had in our backyard. From my childhood I remembered that there used to be a fence around our house. Something that I found particularly interesting was the red soil in Kimberley and Johannesburg. I didn't remember this from my childhood.

I left Kimberley to go back to Johannesburg. Many of my relatives came to see me off at the Kimberley airport and brought me so much food to take on the airplane. I noticed there were army soldiers with guns at the airport. I was nervous. Once I arrived back in Johannesburg I did not have much time to say goodbye to my mother because I went shopping to buy some souvenirs to take back to Canada. The time came to say good-bye to my mother. I was not allowed to enter her hospital room. I was told that there were rows of beds in one very large hall. Only one psychiatrist came once a month to visit all the patients in the asylum. It was devastating for me to discover how my mother had lived for over twenty years. It was so painful to realise how much she suffered. One of the worst things that could ever happen to a woman is to lose her children and have them live halfway around the world not knowing if she will ever see her little ones again.

I felt numb with so much pain for my mother. A nurse brought my mother out into the waiting room. My last visit with my mother was very brief because I was running late to catch my flight back to Canada. My mother's last words to me were, "Good bye." That is all she said to me. I hugged my mother. It was heartbreaking. What was worse was that I had to leave her there. I was twenty eight years old.

When I came back to Canada my father asked me how my mother was. I told him she was not well at all. I really did not want to talk about my trip. I wanted to forget it completely because parts of it were too traumatic and painful for me. Words cannot describe how I felt. My father talked to me for about five minutes about my mother over the telephone. This was the *only* conversation I have ever had in my *entire* life with my father. He said he did not want to talk about my mother anymore. I sensed my father was hurting and I realised that at one point in my parent's lives they must have loved each other. I never talked about my trip to anyone, not even my husband. I continued to write to my mother even though sometimes she did not respond.

I stopped talking to my father for a long time until my sister called me and told me that my father was very sick. I went to his apartment where my sister met me. I told her we needed to call an ambulance because I thought he had had a stroke. The paramedics came and they asked my father if he knew who they were. My father said, "Yes, the police." One of the paramedics said, "It is easy to confuse us because of the uniform we are wearing." My father refused to go with the paramedics to the hospital and they said they could not force him. However, my father did agree to see his family doctor in the morning.

Monday morning came and I went to my father's apartment with my brother and Uncle John to drive my father to the doctor. The doctor talked very nicely to my father and told him he needed to go to the hospital to see why he was losing so much weight. At the hospital I saw how much weight my father had lost. His skin was practically drooping off of him. My brother and I stayed all day with my father until he was admitted into hospital. My father thanked both my brother and me for staying with him. A few days later I received a telephone call from my sister. She said the doctor told her that my father had less than 3 months to live because he had cancer.

Within two weeks my father died. It was June 16, 1993. My father was only 70 years old. He suffered with tremendous pain with his cancer. In 1996, my mother died in South Africa. My mother died in the asylum. I also discovered that mother was raped in that horrible place.

I was only in my mid-thirties when both of my parents died. I did not know either one of them on a *personal level*. I did not have the capacity to grieve or care for my parents until many years later. My healing and forgiveness came too late for them.

Community Bible Church

CHAPTER 13

*"For I was hungry and you gave me something to eat,
I was thirsty and you gave me something to drink,
I was a stranger and you invited me in, I needed
clothes and you clothed me, I was sick and you looked
after me."*

Matthew 25:35-36

In 1998, my friend Lynn from a church in Bradford, Ontario invited me to a one day Women's Bible Retreat at Community Bible Church (The Campus) in Aurora, Ontario. *My journey of recovery, wellness and forgiveness began at this church.* Finding myself at forty years old and not working put me in a severe *crisis mode*. I knew I needed help desperately in order to *survive* in this world. I met a woman by the name of Gabriela in the bathroom at church. As I poured out my heart to her, she handed me a pamphlet on a Women's Recovery Bible Study called "Free Me to Live" by Pastor Ken Freeman. The Recovery Bible

Study was in a group setting with other women and was held at another woman's home named Bonnie. It was a sixteen week course that taught us about God, repentance, forgiveness, and restoration, but most importantly, accepting Christ as our personal Saviour.

I felt there was no hope for me with all the mistakes that I had made in the past. However, I wanted to be *free*. Free from all this tremendous pain and suffering caused by both my parents that was stored up inside of me since early childhood. I made a commitment to attend this Recovery Bible Study for sixteen weeks. I was unsure what to expect in this Recovery Bible Study. Bonnie's home was decorated so beautifully and lit with candles. The atmosphere was soothing, making it more comfortable for us to share our personal and private stories of our past hurts. Sometimes we had the Recovery Bible Study at Gabriela's beautiful home. Gabriela had a bird that would always talk and interrupt us while we were talking. That was because the bird was a male!

The first few weeks of the "Free Me to Live" Bible study were extremely difficult and grueling. Digging up my past was very traumatic for me. Along with reading Scriptures, and working through a workbook, I also had homework to complete. Discussions and friendships developed in the group. We were taught to *let go* of our past hurts.

I found reading the Scriptures for the first time very foreign to me. There were a lot of tears, tremendous pain, laughter and frustrations as we shared our personal stories. Opening up for the first time about my disturbing past became *the first stepping stone to inner healing in my life.* It was at the end of the Recovery Bible Study that I accepted Christ into my heart. From this time forward my life began to change.

However, the wounds of the past continued to fester which led me into Christian counselling. Pastor David Payne recommended that I seek therapy immediately. In therapy I discovered that I had been stuffing my emotions and feelings deep inside for years. I was unable to cry. My past continued to haunt me and that kept me from moving forward with my life. It was too painful for me to talk about my mother.

I shared with the group that I had harboured enormous hatred, bitterness, anger and resentment toward my father. This kept me in bondage for 40 years. The hatred and resentment controlled my life. I had a spirit of bitterness and unforgiveness. Later on, I discovered that God wanted me to open the door of forgiveness in order for me to love again. Yet this took many years of hard work. The wounds had sunken deep within my soul.

I remember Pastor David Payne saying to me one day, "Glendyn, let God take care of your father. Leave it up to Him. Give him up to God." But, I did not know *how* to do this at the time. *I was still suffering emotionally.* My entire family's life was destroyed. My mother's, my siblings and *almost* mine. I found out that this was a *generational curse.* I needed to break this *cycle of abuse.*

I attended Community Bible Church on and off for almost ten years which was very difficult at times for me as well as for the leaders and pastors. It was hard for them to understand someone coming from such an unsafe and unhealthy dysfunctional background. Yet, as compassionate, loving and gracious as they were, they took me under their wing.

I was very stubborn and rebellious with a very fiery verbal nature at first after dealing with so much violence in my past. Since my birth back in South Africa and continuing into Canada for twenty-one years, I experienced first-hand the evil that came to make its home on our doorstep and in our home. *Loneliness* for a little girl to experience and endure until adulthood was *Satan's stronghold against me.*

Years ago Pastor David Payne said to me, *"Glendyn, I don't think you even believe that God loves you."* I never forgot those words and even today it rings in my ears loud and clear. In the past I felt I was unlovable and I had a hard time believing how anyone could love me, even God. I realized that God wanted me to serve out my life doing something good. That He has a purpose and plan for my life. In Jeremiah 29:11: *"For I know the plans I have for you,"* declares the Lord, *"Plans to prosper you and not to harm you, plans to give you hope and a future."*

Bonnie, Gabriela, and Alison from "Free Me to Live" Recovery Bible Study became my mentors over a ten year period with the assistance of their spouses as well as the pastors at my church. Studying the Scriptures took discipline and training. Meditating on the knowledge of the Bible soothed me through my darkest hours, especially during those awful lonely nights that I often suffered through. Pastor David and Pastor Stephen were very patient and kind with me. I went to them for guidance and counselling.

In September of 1999 after "Free Me to Live" Recovery Bible Study, I went back to school and took the Personal Support Worker program. This program trained me how to care for and assist seniors and the elderly in the community as well as in a long term care facility. I concentrated on my studies instead of wallowing in self pity over the past. I worked full time and attended evening classes twice a week. It was very demanding going to school *and* working full time. There were times I would work twelve hours at my job then I would go to night school.

One evening I was late for night school. I did not have time to go home and take a shower and change my clothes. I opened the door to the classroom. Everyone, including the teacher, looked at me. I said, "I am here!" The class burst out laughing because I looked like a lion with my wet hair sticking up. I was wearing a ragged old jacket with the sleeves too long, covering my hands.

The teacher said, "Let me help you to your seat." She took my arm and led me to my seat. Now my classmates roared even louder with laughter. She turned to the classroom and said, "This is what I call dedication!" My friend beside me said to me while still laughing, "Don't come to class like that again!" I just ignored her. I also had to participate in field placement every Saturday mornings for training from 7 a.m. to 2:30 p.m. in a long-term care facility. I also started Christian counselling again. I moved around a lot, living in basement apartments. I just felt there was no place to call *"home."*

However, *God never gave up on me.* In 2001, I managed to graduate from the Personal Support Worker Program with high honours. I had reconciled with my husband. He took photographs with me and my friends along with one of my teachers at our graduation ceremony. The sun was shining and it was a good day.

On November 30, 2003, I was baptized. This day was a symbol of putting on the new, renewed me. It meant I am a new creation in Christ Jesus and all of my past sins are washed away. My brother and oldest sister came to see me getting baptized. It was a new experience for me and for them to see me baptized.

The Scripture verse that Bonnie left with me when I received my baptismal was: "When your mother and father forsake you the Lord will take care of you." For the second reading, Gabriela recited Proverbs 3:5-6: "Trust in the Lord with all your heart and lean not on your own understanding; in all your ways acknowledge him, and he will make your paths straight."

During the course of my attending "Free Me to Live" Recovery Bible Study, I had to change my psychiatrist of eighteen years. The distance was too far for me to travel to his office. My new psychiatrist could not figure me out. He said that there was nothing wrong with me. I asked him a few months later in another session. "Can you tell me what my diagnosis is?" He said he did not know yet. After 20 years of being diagnosed and labelled with Schizophrenia, he told me that I was *misdiagnosed*. He diagnosed me with many different disorders. At the time I had injured my back and I could not work so this psychiatrist wanted me to live in a *group home.* I refused because this would take me many steps backwards. My psychiatrist was so angry with me because I did not want to live in a group home. I decided to get another opinion. Bonnie and her husband Barry from the "Free Me to Live" Recovery Bible Study were so very kind to take me in for the summer. Later, I moved in with my brother in downtown Toronto.

I mentioned to Gabriela from the Recovery Bible Study that even though I moved so many times, my small personal Bible that I had received back in 1969 at church kept on appearing. It ended up in my apartment again. God was *tracking* me down. Imagine that! He was pursuing me even though I kept on rejecting Him and ignoring Him. I did not want to hear anything about Jesus. One day I opened up this small Bible and to my surprise it had my Uncle John and Aunty Pete's address in it from when we first came to Canada. Both of them were church-going people and knew the Bible inside out. This brought back so many fond memories of living with them. I thought to myself, "Is God trying to tell me something?" But, I put the Bible away again in my dresser drawer. I forgot about it. I kept on running from the Cross. I was running from God. I had fear about my future and I kept on looking back on my past. I became crippled and trapped by my past. I lived in a barren place. It is such a lonely place.

My walk with the Lord was still young. One hot summer day I was in my brother's apartment. I heard a voice. The voice said, *"Take control of your life."* I looked around the room. I thought to myself, "Pastor David is following me." I tried to run away from him. Pastor David said the exact same words to me before I left Community Bible Church, now called The Campus. I did not realize that it was *God*. After two months of living with my brother, I moved into my own apartment with a middle aged couple, a pastor and his wife.

After the move, I started reliving my past in South Africa and my unsafe childhood. At the time I did not know that this was a symptom of Post Traumatic Stress Disorder. I went for help at a hospital. I was able to find part-time work. I just started this job but had to take some time off. I became physically ill from the move.

One night while sitting in a coffee shop in Toronto, I started to write a letter to my Aunty Milly in South Africa. I wrote that I wanted to come home to South Africa for good. I tore up the letter instead and walked home into the dark lonely night, crying. When I arrived home I cried, sobbing my heart out uncontrollably while lying on the couch feeling very much alone in my apartment. All the pain that I had suffered after all the years of abuse, neglect and abandonment was coming to the surface. It was Christmastime. I spent it alone. I must have drifted off to sleep. I was awoken with the sound of a loud bolt of thunder followed by a very powerful and authoritative *male voice* that spoke to me. The voice said very loudly,

"Stop suffering!" Startled, I instantly woke up. I jumped out of my bed. I started making my bed quickly. The voice spoke to me again and said, **"Go feed the poor!"** I was *shocked*. I was absolutely in wonder and awe. That is when I *knew*.

I instantly telephoned Pastor David Payne from Community Bible Church (now called The Campus) in Aurora from Toronto that same day. I told Pastor David what happened. I said, "It is true." *"There is a God!"* I told Pastor David what the voice said to me. Pastor David said, *"Yes, then you must be obedient and go feed the poor all day long, Glendyn."* I also telephoned Bonnie from my "Free Me to Live" Bible study to tell her about my experience. I was so happy. It was only a few days later that I noticed that there was a change in me. It was a *miracle*. My injured back was totally *healed*. I felt no pain. *God healed my back.* It was from this day forward that I believed *there is a God* and that He totally loves me. *Somebody actually loves me.* I promised myself that I was going to be obedient to God.

In December 2004, I went to the Day Treatment Program at the hospital in North York where I attended group therapy. This group therapy was facilitated by a healthcare professional. One day in group therapy I actually cried for the first time for both my parents. I said in the group, *"I miss my mom and my dad."* There were actually tears in my eyes for them. I felt heartbroken that I had no parents. A few days later, I was in the grocery store. I began having *flashbacks* about when I was twelve years old. I dropped the groceries crying. I ran home. I stopped this memory from surfacing. I was afraid I was going to find out something horrific.

When I went to the Day Treatment program the next day I began bringing it up. I was told not to talk about my past because there were others with more severe mental health issues in the group. I felt it was a part of my healing process. I felt that I needed to get to the *root* of my problem which was my childhood abuse. I needed *talk therapy.*

I started to research into community resources in Toronto and York Region which would assist me on my wellness journey and recovery. I was able to work at my part-time job assisting a woman confined to a wheelchair who was a quadriplegic with cerebral palsy in her home. I also attended the Day Treatment Program at the same time. It was not easy. I was determined to work hard and get the help that I needed. This program at the hospital taught me about medications, relaxation techniques, psychotherapy, women's issues and other topics. All of these groups were crucial toward my journey of wellness.

Life was extremely difficult for me. Yes, I *struggled.* I made a decision that I was going to take back my life. I never let my mental illness or my past stop me from becoming a success in life. I worked very hard on myself. I shared my story with my peers and some of my friends. I focused my wellness on my strengths only, having a positive attitude, taking the focus off myself by helping others, being involved in advocate work, volunteering, and making people laugh. My wellness is being productive and contributing to society.

The most important decision I ever made was that I was going to listen and follow the advice, counsel, and the teachings of my pastors and mentors. I found that by having a close relationship with our Lord Jesus, reading the Bible, and meditating upon and memorizing Scripture taught me how to handle life's issues. This all became the source of my strength, comfort and abundance of joy. Rich blessings began pouring into my life from God. I took "Free Me to Live" Recovery Bible Study four times to help me recapture my identity and be restored from my past. I eventually *"let go"* which was an extremely difficult and lengthy process. Healing, restoration, forgiveness and reconciliation finally came.

God shaped and moulded me into the woman that I have become today. *A woman with morals, spiritual values, focused on helping others.* I will never forget the goodness, grace, generosity, kindness and vast emotional support that this church showed me in my time of desperation. Shortly after, in another Bible study in Toronto my forgiveness for my father evolved. Luke 1:37 says, "For nothing is impossible with God."

The Power of Forgiveness

"If you, O Lord, kept a record of sins, O Lord, who could stand? But with you there is forgiveness; therefore you are feared."

Psalm 130:3-4

In September 2005, I attended a program called the Living Waters Program at Evangel Temple in Toronto. One day as we prayed, I asked God, *"God, please forgive my father."* I finally released my father to God. *This released me as well.* This was an extremely huge step for me. Immediately, I felt the chains of bondage were broken. I had been trapped in darkness for many years. Now, I was able to see the light. By the grace of God I finally forgave my father for destroying our family. It took me forty years to forgive my father. I truly believe forgiveness is a process, a daily process. It does not happen instantly. I could not believe that even God could take my pain away. He said to me, *"Glendyn, it is finished." "It is over." "I will carry your pain."*

When I worked with seniors in long-term care facilities and in the community I saw that there were so many seniors being left alone. *No one visits them.* The Bible teaches us that we should respect our elderly people. I felt shame and sadness that I was unable to have a relationship with my father. I would have wanted to know about his rich heritage in South Africa. I also would have travelled to South Africa more often to help ease my poor mother's pain. But, I did not have the capacity to do this. My healing came too late. Now, both of them are gone. I was in my mid-thirties when I lost both my parents.

As I became a mature woman, I realized and understood that it was a huge responsibility for my father to raise four children as a single parent. As a new immigrant leaving a country such as South Africa, his native homeland, my father left all the years of experience and all of his successes behind. He left his people, family and friends. I know that it was very difficult for my father to come to a new country and start all over again. My father did what he could. His upbringing was far more incomprehensible than I could ever imagine.

> *I miss both my parents today. Not knowing them. "For I will forgive their wickedness and will remember their sins no more."*
>
> *Jeremiah 31: 33*

Life After Fifty

"Ask the former generations and find out what their fathers learned, for we were born only yesterday and know nothing, and our days on earth are but a shadow. Will they not instruct you and tell you? Will they not bring forth words from their understanding?"

Job 8:8-10

In 2010, I was informed that Schizophrenia was an incorrect diagnosis and my final diagnosis was *Post Traumatic Stress Disorder*. This disorder is about having flashbacks of the past, panic attacks, anxiety, and nightmares.

I had an injustice imposed upon me through many tragedies and losses beginning in South Africa and on into Canada; more than the average human being. But, God restored the years that were stolen from me with a bright rainbow for my future. I had to learn that a lot of people will not accept me in society because of my past and because I have a mental illness. *The Lord told me that people will still see me through my past and not see what God has done in my life.*

My dear Aunty Pete would always say to me, *"Glendyn, the devil takes care of his own."* The last letter written to me by my Aunty Milly in South Africa at ninety years old read, *"Don't forget to say your prayers daily, Glendyn."* My Aunty Iris in South Africa before she passed away in March, 2012 said to me, *"God is good, Glendyn!"*

I miss all those who are gone now as they taught me what was important in life. I have discovered that I developed special traits from both of my parents. I see my parents in a different light now. My father did not know any better. Both of my parents did what they could in that generation. I love both of my parents today. I think of them often. Through my late Uncle John I have discovered that my father worked hard at making a difference in this world. He tried to make a better place for his people and his children. Both of my parents made a decision for us children to have a better life living in Canada. I have found a place to finally call *"home."* I am very proud to be a *Canadian* but I have not forgotten my *"roots"* either. The first fifty years were definitely a mountain to climb. I had to learn that my worth and my value are in Jesus Christ. Life is so much easier now.

I had to learn to forgive. In Mathew 6:15 the Bible says that if you do not forgive, your Heavenly Father will not forgive you. Most importantly, *I had to learn to forgive myself.* I also forgave that man who raped and sexually abused me. *I had to forgive everyone.* Once I had learned forgiveness, all the shame and guilt were washed away by the blood of Jesus. At last healing came. Isaiah 61:7 says, *"Instead of their shame my people will receive a double portion, and instead of disgrace they will rejoice in their inheritance; and so they will inherit a double portion in their land, and everlasting joy will be theirs."*

On March 8, 2012, my friend Sandy and I found ourselves back at the Salvation Army Evangeline Residence in Toronto, Ontario. I rang the bell. The big door that once welcomed me years ago opened. As soon as I entered, I noticed the red carpet had been replaced by wooden floors. The front foyer was also replaced by a huge front desk. I spoke to the staff and I told them that I once was a resident back in 1981. I was introduced to all the staff. I felt humbled and honoured to be taken on a tour of the residence. This residence was once a safe haven that I took refuge in thirty four years ago. A lot has changed but I remembered a little while walking along the hallways and through the rooms. The dining area was still familiar but the kitchen area had been renovated. The chapel was moved down to the lower level. Today, there are programs and counselling for the women living at the shelter. I feel that these programs and counselling are all crucial and are a very positive step for the women in the residence.

I could tell that the upstairs desperately needed a makeover but funds were very limited. I knew that one day I was going to give back to this residence that offers hope and a helping hand to better the lives of women at risk. I thanked the staff at the end of the tour. I can honestly say today that I was very fortunate and feel truly blessed that I have had the opportunity to walk on "the red carpet." Philippians 4:13 reads, "I can do all things through Christ who gives me strength."

Today, I have peace because Jesus is in my heart. God touched my heart with His love. I found happiness at last. My inner strength and the resilience that I developed as a little girl but most importantly my faith in God pulled me through all this.

Today, I feel like I am the most blessed person on this earth. I have received many blessings from our Heavenly Father. I am finally happy! Yes, I had a bad start in life but the finish will definitely be a good one. I became a "Psychiatric Survivor." In Romans 8:28 it reads: *"And we know that in all things God works for the good of those who love Him, who have been called according to His purpose."*

"Having looked the beast of the past in the eyes, having asked and received forgiveness…let us shut the door of the past – not to forget it – but to allow it not to in prison us."

        -Archbishop Desmond Tutu, South Africa

21ˢᵗ April, 1967

To Whom It May Concern

I have known and worked with Him for the past twenty-seven years, and have been Secretary to him in our foremost South African Coloured Cricket Association, and also in the Diamond Fields Cricket Union, both of which he has been President for many years now. He is a highly respected Commissioner of Oaths.

And he remembered this, displaying that wooden plaque proudly on his bedroom wall in the country in which he hoped to win for him, his children and his people for their freedom and a new life.

This man has impressed me with his initiative, diligence, perseverance and integrity in every thing he undertakes, and these qualities have always brought his success.

And he remembered this, putting a roof over their heads with food and clothing.

This man has been a loyal, competent and an efficient employee of the De Beers Consolidated Mines Ltd., where he is still employed, and where his services are greatly valued. Seeking to create a better world, he is the organizer of all social functions, and our community holds him in very high esteem, because he is the leading official of over fourteen welfare organizations, as well as being the Chairman of the Transvaal Road Primary School, Chairman of the Thistles Rugby Club, Chairman of the Beaconsfield Wanderers Cricket Club and auditor of the South African Rugby Union.

And he remembered this, talking each Friday night with his older brother of the old country and the family and friends who were still there.

His untiring efforts in the administration and organizing of all functions and events that lead to the educational and cultural uplift of his community have always been successful, because he is a born organizer and administrator, with a pleasing and attractive, yet forceful personality.

Coming from a very highly respected family, he is a loyal and devoted member of the Anglican Church, where his services on various committees of the church are very much appreciated.

He will be a grave *loss* to a community that loses him, and a very valuable gain to one that accepts him. He bears with him my personal best wishes for every success in the future.

And he lived this, each day.

To My Mother and Father

"Please forgive me. I love you both dearly.
May you both rest in peace."

For you created my inmost being; you knit me together in my mother's womb. I praise you because I am fearfully and wonderfully made; your works are wonderful, I know that full well. My frame was not hidden from you when I was made in the secret place.

Psalm 139:13-15

My mother, Blanche Francke Kester, holding my oldest sister Lynette, at her birthday party. Kimberley, South Africa.

In my mother's arms at my birthday party, with Lynette.
Kimberley, South Africa.

Family photo at the De Beers Diamond Mining Company Christmas Party. Kimberley, South Africa.
(Back row: Blanche Francke Kester, Norman Kester, Sr.; middle row: Glendyn Kester, Lynette Kester; front row: Norman Kester, Jr., Rosemary Kester.)

*Our family home: 28 Aster Road, Square Hill Park,
Kimberley, South Africa.*

My father's sister, Aunty Milly, and I.

Uncle John, my father's brother, influenced me at ten years of age, and taught me that education is the road to success.

Recommendations

SPIRITUAL

Put your *"Trust in God"*

1. Pray daily.
2. Read your Bible, devotional and inspirational books. *Renew* your mind daily with memorizing and meditating on Scripture.
3. I suggest a place of worship (church) that you feel comfortable with.
4. Make an appointment to see the pastor and confide in your pastor.
5. Become involved in your church, join a Bible study, a small group.
6. Seek Christian counselling. There are some Christian Therapists that will take you on a sliding scale financially.
7. Work through your past then let it go, forgive those who have offended you.

8. Watch ministries on television: Journal daily on the ministries and the positive activities you did that day.
9. When you feel lonely, stressed, or depressed, listen to uplifting worship music.
10. Read self-help books, autobiographies, biographies.
11. Only see the good in people.
12. Encourage one another and lift others up!
13. Count your blessings every day.
14. *Sing and give thanks to the Lord for whatever you have and with whatever you are doing.*

YOUR MENTAL HEALTH AND WELL-BEING
Friends are a true *"Gift from God"*

1. **Accept** that you have a mental illness, seek help, then work on only your strengths.
2. Do **not** discontinue your medications unless you consult with your doctor.
3. Memorize the names and dosages of your medications.
4. Educate yourself on your illness and medication.
5. Listen to your body with your medications.
6. Reward yourself for getting out of bed, this is a big accomplishment.
7. Have a support system in place, tap into community supports and services.
8. You may need a Case Manager.
9. Do not become dependent on your psychiatrist, healthcare professionals, or others.

10. Take responsibility for your own life.
11. Make healthy choices; the right moral choices.
12. Be independent and be positive.
13. Surround yourself with positive people.
14. Set healthy boundaries.
15. Attend workshops on assertiveness training, self esteem, anger management, financial literacy, stress reduction, relaxation techniques, yoga, art therapy, learn a new craft.
16. Join a self help group, read self-help books.

STAYING HEALTHY
"A busy person is a happy person"

1. Eat healthy – fruit, vegetables, poultry, fish, red meat, grain breads, nuts.
2. Take vitamins daily, ask your pharmacist/doctor for recommendations.
3. Grocery shop with a budget: check weekly flyers on sales at different stores, clip coupons.
4. If you do not know how to cook, follow an easy recipe or take a cooking class.
5. Use the internet, library, book stores, your home church for community resources.
6. Get enough sleep – 8 hours per night regularly, have a little nap in the afternoon.
7. Get some fresh air, sunshine almost every day.
8. Exercise at home either alone or with a partner to music, walking is cheap.

9. Talk to people, connect with people. (eg: A mall, on the bus, on the street)
10. **_Sing_**, do a little dance.
11. Help a senior, take them for a walk, visit them/carry their groceries, send them a card, give them a telephone call.
12. Volunteer with an organization/find employment or go back to school.
13. Learn a new hobby, join a fun dance class, knitting, crochet or wood working.
14. Nurture and love yourself, pamper yourself with a bath, have a facial or a massage.
15. Buy a plant, adopt a pet, cat, dog, bird or a fish and take care of them.
16. Be the very best person you can. If you have failed you could have succeeded.
17. Do not compare yourself to others or what others have.
18. **_Smile_**, the world will smile back.
19. **_Laughter is the best medicine._**
20. Don't Give Up! Look Up to the Heavens and smile!

THE SINNER'S PRAYER

I invite you to pray the "Sinner's Prayer" and tell someone at a church.

> *"Lord Jesus please come into my heart, and into my life.*
> *Please forgive me for my sins*
> *Thank you for the solid rock I stand on*
> *Amen"*
>
> *1 John 1:12*

About the Author

Ms. Kester was born in South Africa and at the age of ten her father moved her and her three siblings to Canada.

Ms. Kester became a psychiatric survivor working through her issues by succeeding in education, employment and most importantly, her faith in God. She obtained 3 diplomas and 14 certificates in various disciplines. She has worked for 31 years. Ms. Kester is a speaker, author and an advocate.

She was interviewed twice by her local paper with York Region Media Group to break mental health barriers.

Ms. Kester is a member of the Canadian Mental Health Association of York Region Branch. She volunteered in their Family Education Groups and at their Speaker's Bureau. Ms. Kester co-facilitates groups at the Krasman Centre in Richmond Hill, Ontario, for their Family Education Drop-In Support Groups.

She was married for 22 years and now lives independently in a lovely apartment in Newmarket, Ontario with her adorable cat BooBoo.

CPSIA information can be obtained at www.ICGtesting.com
Printed in the USA
LVOW13s1037121013

356572LV00009B/48/P

CPSIA information can be obtained at www.ICGtesting.com
Printed in the USA
LVOW13s1037121013

356572LV00009B/48/P